MW01127304

The Theatre and *The Temple Over the Canyon*, Segesta, Italy by Joseph Pennell (1915)

A Lawless

People

Cynicism and America's

System of Laws

J. D. Stewart

To Fred and Mitchell

Cover photo provided by iStock.com (#39649930).
Frontispiece provided by fromoldbooks.com,
The Theatre and *The Temple Over the Canyon*, Segesta,
Italy by Joseph Pennell," In the Land of Temples
(1915).
ISBN -13 978-1502339591
ISBN -10 1502339595

Justice is turned away backward, and righteousness stands afar off; for truth is fallen in the street, and uprightness can't enter. Yes, truth is lacking; and he who departs from evil makes himself a prey. Yahweh saw it, and it displeased him who there was no justice. He saw that there was no man, and wondered that there was no intercessor:

- Isaiah 59:14-16, *World English Bible*

Preface

Segesta was an ancient fortress. High in the mountains of Sicily, and overlooking a valley which offered protection to its citizens. With roads giving controlled access to the city and despite its high prominence which favored Segesta under attack, it had a protracted history of losses to invaders. At one point in its history Segesta negotiatiated for alliance which gave up its Sicilian heritage to become Greek by choice and possibly by neglect, from Segestan to Athenian. Ultimately the city was deserted. Having been established in roughly 1200 B.C., it came to ruin after being inhabited many centuries later by Arabs and Vandals. Not only did the citizens forsake the city and gave away it native identity, but it gave up its heritage never to be re-inhabited by those steeped in Segestan culture which would thus be lost for all time.

This city, protected by natural barriers, obviously did little to protect its culture and was ultimately destroyed. Rules, laws and mores serve, if adequately defended, to ward off the degrading invasion of cultural conflict and national insouciance. It is not the influx of cultures, however, that sidelines national determination, nor the émigrés who are expectantly searching for stability and hope. The main threat to our rights is the lawless obedience of citizens to the prevailing legal constraints that define our culture by setting its limits. To lose those constraints, to not oppose outside forces or to decline defense of internal laws and values and remembering Segesta suggests that cultures may become overrun by a lack of concern for a country's culture and laws which have define it.

America is facing that sort of alienation from its culture and its laws. It is interesting that the resilience of our country to decolonization and the defeat of slavery, an internal threat to democracy, seems now to be falling to another inward threat, a failure to keep laws and respect for those under its rule. This project has been undertaken to consider this internal defection. And although globalization can be blamed for our disaffection, even a strident rebellion against the values and practices by which we have been united as a nation and through which we have been civilized, our moving away from core understandings of who we are is at our own behest. Segesta used trickery to gain the favor of the Greeks which shows a willingness to abandon their cultural values to become Athenian. Fearing that Segesta was not rich enough to warrant its takeover Segesta began building a temple, a sign of wealth, but Segesta was not wealthy, and once Athens had the city among its conquestt, the work on the temple was abandoned. For us its is not simply that we have brought in different peoples, for we are a nation of people seeking hope from all parts of the world, but we have ceased to be the people that our tradition valued. This could and may have happened to other cities and countries in the past, but our national defenses are greater than high mountains and deep valleys. Yet, although we may be militarily secure at present, we must defend against the slippage in our own code of honor as a law abiding citizenry.

And now as we reckon current cultural disaffection we must address its causes and possible solutions to what has now become epidemic. But what makes such a writing project worthy of its effort? Is it a lifetime of observation with which the events fit, or could it be that a series of conversations with those that have formulated opinions, especially if they differ from one's own in a free exchange of ideas, could be the impetus for pensive insights? *Ode on a Grecian Urn* was no more than Keats' imaginings, but it had both earthly and eternal implications. C. S. Lewis wrote a book on the critical perusal of another book not to his liking in *The Abolition of Man*. So it is not unimaginable that a book, possibly a worthy book, could be conceived in an extended conversation in which three people each having different understandings about the failed condition of our culture and the prospects for reclamation of modern America could come to grips with the realities of disaffection and consider ways back to a cultural re-dawning.

Sometimes one has the belief that he or she has the potential answer to a pressing problem, maybe not in detail, but proceeds to share it with others. It may or may not receive encouraging support, but it has a voice that is heard which may in the discussion, heated or civil, create an impasse for communication or consensus and agreement. The former almost never occurs in intricate discussion. My two dear friends had very different answers, one perhaps procedural the other more radical and less exculpatory. This small book is an attempt to consider the issues raised mostly from the author's understanding, to parse issues and to consider a way back to a stable culture, one protected from the erosion of values by cultural protections, a way back to a law-abiding society.

The conversation goes on with my friends and, as indeed it goes on all over the nation out of concern for the civility of other nations. It is hoped that one day this society itself will wake not to a proposal for change but for real change that brings a people and peoples to a lawful view of life and the exercise of personal preference weighed against the stability of society.

At this time we are seeing in the Crimea and in the Ukraine a partial willingness to fall back into the culturally disrupted pattern of totalitarian security. Some citizens of these regions parametric to the new Russia want to assume a cultural imperative that is safe and easy but which may not meet the wishes of all concerned and the native reemergent culture. But some are willing to give up who they are, if they can even remember why they were a nation, who they are, to fall into the bed of Procrustus, to be made to fit the wishes of their captors as was Segesta.

Are we to follow the same path, maybe without violence and killing? Will we subject ourselves to a warless attrition handing our nation and souls over to a power of self-sufficiency apart from the laws and rules that have made us who we were? Segesta began building a temple to show the Athenians that they were financially worthy of being taken over, they wanted to be made captive. Will we silently give ourselves and our country to become a Crimean or Ukrainian equivalent, a lap dog for the unleashed power of the wants and desires of a nation, perhaps our own nation, acting self-servingly and being separated from those around us amongst whom have, in part, made us who we are.

We are all unlawful citizens whose very acts of illegality and uncaring push all of us closer to a nation in which we pursue only laws we favor and deny the right of the majority historically to be governed by the laws of the land.

Table of Contents

Introduction

The Old Testament is rife with recounting the anger of God with his children, Israel. He offered them laws as commandments to keep them in his will, but they continued to disobey him and what stood for the practical and defense guidelines for a happy, honest and fair people. God was angry but did not destroy all of mankind, and he allowed the righteous to survive his judgment giving them laws as guidelines to avoid their future trespasses. But he was the Father of a disobedient and stiff-necked people, who would not do what they should and be profited in return. As were these ancient Israelites, we are a lawless people. One that considers laws mere suggestions and pick and choose what to obey and what not to obey. The courts cannot keep up with the flagrant violations of the penal code, but we break many more than we are held accountable finding omission of law the form of modern cultural denial.

Which of our laws do we not honor? Are the laws that we disrespect or break not justifiable as valuable contributions to the legal canon. My friends and I had long discussions about the government and the laws that have been averted by official decree and the type of government that could prevent our leaders from becoming illegal and felonious and would stand top defend and support our legal system. Both Fred and Mitchell in our discussions thought that the lawless were those who accumulated unlawful patterns of action as powerful leaders in the government. Fred felt that there was not option that we must revolt and take back our nation from those in power who had stolen its protection of us and our nation's glory. Mitchell claimed that we might need to tweak our understanding of our form of governmental democracy in order to avoid more disregard for citizen's rights and make democracy a more personal priority. My argument to both Fred and Mitchell was that we are the makers and the keepers of the laws, or we are those that trespass those laws. By disregarding our responsibility to our laws, those who do not keep the laws as citizens or law givers rob law of its power. We are not only no better than our leaders but we are one and the same. We elected them to represent us, and hardly ever raise a challenge to their holding office. The leadership often represent a lawless people, which will be explored in this book, and who could only be expected to be lawless themselves. Our motivation it seems, in all that we do, legally or illegally, is to make our way through life more by our own will than by the rules of society whereby we should at least acquiesce in our responsibility to others.

This understanding of our responsibility to others was of utmost concern when I penned the book *Loss of Others*, how we have lost the sense of others and thereby lost our sense of ourselves as a extension. Flagrant disregard for others must, as it has proven so, become at some point a matter of law. The extent to which we value ourselves and our wishes and wants above others is, in increasing measure, our willingness to not only overlook the needs of others but to disadvantage others beyond the strictures of legality, deciding that something that is not legal is first and foremost fair and caring. Yet the real option awaits our desire to have something regardless of our neighbors will or wish or even safety.

Our elected officials are those that campaigned for our agendas; today, they are a political and social clone of our selfish wishes. If those at the top are found to be breaking the law, then we are responsible for their opportunity to transgress. If we approve, we are culpable. How could we condone such lawlessness? We show in our personal lives illegality by not obeying the speed limit, fudging on tax forms and taking work materials home with us. These may seem small breaches of the law, if considered issues of law at all, but they are, in fact, the foot in the door to more aggressively bend or break the laws that do protect us, our neighbors and our community. Not only have we breached the legal barriers to individual laws, but, due to the interlocking nature of legal protections, we may have produced interstices of weakness among those remaining in a system of law.

I recently saw a parent whose child was killed in one of the school shootings crying about his lost son. He said, "When will these killings stop?" The real question is when will we turn to the law and protect it and not shop it for our preferences. If allowed to do as we will, people will be disadvantaged and people will die. Breaking the speed limit may be a normal activity for most citizens, but when you want your self-inflicted killing to be noticed, one of the most powerful ways to accomplish this suicide is for formerly normal people to kill themselves and to take others withthem. It would then be more difficult for others to ignore you even if you had been ignored during your life by your parents and society, while some from a deep-seeded psychopathy could not have been turned away from avenues of killing and destruction induced by nature or nurture. Law breaking under conditions of desperation and no recompense for a final act becomes a dramatic expression of pain or disregard in a tortured existence. In most cases it is hard to believe that the young man who committed these killings had not picked and chosen laws to violate in his young life. Entry level violation of laws like smoking dope or breaking the speed limit, where unlike others, this is where the trespass stopped, had been respected and consistently enforced, these patterns of illegality might not have been explored if these killers had been raised on the respect for non-negotiable guidelines called laws.

One of the issues that must be considered in law breaking is an understanding of evil. Why should young people indiscriminately take the lives of others, which unlike acts of passion, bear malice to those killed but also the desire to destroy the potentially happy lives of others and their families? Perhaps it is taking from others what the perpetrator has never felt, that he or she has never experienced. Where does this cold, deadly and phlegmatic lawlessness and evil begin? We know where it might end. In the hands of a nation whose people have no respect for the guiding laws we may speculate on a end.

Chapter 1

Lawlessness

Evil

Evil is said to be either natural or man-made. Tornadoes, tsunamis, volcanic activity are natural and involve no direct acts of man, but moral evils are the carried out will of man for his own purpose without concern or care of others. Natural evils are often seen as God failing man and allowing nature to interrupt the daily happiness of life. At times floods and area fires reveal man's complicity in the resultant devastation. There is the idea that God let such horrors kill and destroy, while man may escape prosecution or exonerated for his hand in the carnage. God falls victim to those that deny his existence receiving scolding and rebuff for what is conveniently seen as his failure to be a God to his people. God becomes a handy out when man is made to bear responsibility. Once in a conversation an acquaintance told that he had come to disbelieve in God having seen how little children with catastrophic diseases suffered at a children's hospital. But these are sometimes environmental perturbations created by man and he had no way of separating the causes into natural, God caused, and man-made diseases. Some children were injured by parents or in home accidents, but God received my friends rebuke. It would seem by inference that God often reaps the blame when even those that commit crimes against children do not believe in him and scoffers blame him while giving byes to the perpetrator as if evil were some organic and unavoidable force which takes people who have no ability to avoid their actions. Others claim that all of society is to blame since we have influenced their actions and therefore bear responsibility. It would even seem that because God is not in our face due to his spiritual nature, we hang what is clearly man's doing on him, for his lack of proximity. Overall man does not necessarily receive credit for evil motivation for which He has proven, supposedly, through unjust wars and famine; He is responsible.

The point here is that man is also capable, by himself, of horrific acts. This is possible in anyone of us. When a Jewish man visited Nuremberg after the second world war to see the monster Eichmann who was involved in the killing of Jews, he expected to see a grotesque monster, but only saw a man like himself. We have proven that we are capable, as men and women, of horrendous acts of evil. Theodicy is the best version of a good God and man's tendency to flaunt the ability to compromise good for evil purposes.

Philosophy and Moral Culpability

Our philosophic moorings have changed in action in the last several centuries. Socrates, Plato and Aristotle may have been concerned about the common good, but we have left much of that consideration far behind in modern times for an actionable life. We need only to return to Nietzsche and his summary of mankind. Each man is either a master or a slave, and the relative power evoked by each will naturally make that distinction clear. No one wants to be a slave so the determination is clear, dominate others. Exert your will and crush others. This may be done in finance, politics, any career and any occasion. Domination is your responsibility over everything and everyone.

Although more subtile is the philosophical ideas of Hegel who influenced Nietzsche. He saw truth as a fleeting replaceable obstacle to the exertion of power. No common knowledge was made to stand, no common event was terminal. Life today is only to be replaced by the events of tomorrow. Understandings of the world are in flux and will be replaced by the new tomorrow. And although Hegel believed in an ultimate finality, an absolutism in which an equilibrium of balanced replacement would yield to an idealistic end, his legacy would fall to John Dewey, America's pragmatist, who believed that this replacement did not end. Man had no true identity nor was their truth, fixed and indisputable. Man, healthy man, could be in the throes of the process of change all the time and therefore had no definitive character to be seen as good or evil. Man could possibly only upon death be judged and probably not then, with no one's honor raised from the dead finding definitive glory. Dewey's contribution was that the replaceability of character was given in consideration of the person who was capable of becoming something different, could become something better or something worse. Dewey's meliorism offset the possible pessimistic proposal by favoring man with idealistic and wishful thoughts that man would on the whole do better overtime but not to the end of perfection. The overall effect of Dewey ala Hegel was that of uncertainty forever. Uncertainty about the world around and even uncertainty about the self and its nature and necessarily his view of laws.

Dewey also gave to America, not that his only influence was in our nation, a Kantian idea that was to change more of what most had considered common and sensical. Each understanding of each event was individual and could not with confidence be transferred to others. Two or more people see an accident and each could have different yet equally right understandings of the event. All knowledge had the perspective of each observer and the primary observer, that is each person, had a viable and indisputable understanding of the event.

If each understanding was valid, replaceable then, there would be no definitive understanding about the accident, no necessary culpability, no necessary sequential events leading up to and through the crash and potential deaths. This causes not just a moral problem but a legal one as well. This result was an unintended difficulty, I would imagine, by Dewey. He was said to have struggled into his last days with the consequential issues that arose from viable individual authority which he saw as ultimately selfish, the accordance of the role of master. Unpurterbed by the ultimate failure of his giving the individual the ultimate power over definitive observation he wrote that even if he saw the gun smoking, pointing at the victim, his judgment of homicidal causation would not be sure.

Is there not some evil in formulating the understandings of events without a definite and common history. No consensus for the jury. And the point here is that we must be able to resolve issues of culpability, right or wrong, good and evil. These ideas, on the contrary, promoted by Dewey's philosophy and related philosophies that followed over the last hundred plus years, have gradually crept into our psyche and left us easily given to our own power of understanding and our own view of morality, each of which is no longer understood to begin with our motivation for action, but seems to be an externalized quality. We talk today of the immorality of polluting the rivers and the air, the making of vast fortunes while others find not enough to eat. These are often undesirable or even reprehensible acts of deprivation that have found their evil, if you will, in related acts of purposeful deprivation. Motivation, was disdained by Dewey as he felt that the inner feeling and outer action could not necessarily be shown to be causal except possibly after the action, but this was not a certainty. This leaves the act to stand not of intent and outcome but to be evaluated by outcome alone. If for no other reason, motivation removed from consideration, the law could only find guilt not for provocation not extenuation of circumstance for any illegal act. Since, for instance, a homicide could not be ruled justifiable or flagrant, excusable or inexcusable, then, by this reasoning, we must acquit. Did we run a red light, should we be fined or let off for lack of surety that you did, in fact, violate the law. If you say that you did not run the light, no secondary objection could be raised and would not successfully counter your primary observation. In this way law has been made the object of our feeling as motivation has been judged, for want of a different term, unsure.

Purpose of the Law

As a result of these changes increasingly finding their way into the American understanding of the world, clear objective lines of personal responsibility and even legality are called into question. The fear is that if we are all capable of horrific acts and are now without clear issues of motivation are all acts to be judged by the most rigorous understanding or will we be excused for unexplainable intent? And, knowing that our actions may not be able to be judged for malice, to what extent will we go to exert our power, our individual understanding and self justification. Motivation removed, little can be said of the insignificance of minor acts and the significance of felonies. They all must subject to questioning and dismissal. Evil can be in the mind before if can be borne out in action. If we cannot at least explore the motivation for action, then we and others could be living bombs ready to be activated. Falling back on our previous example, this could be what we have seen in the school killings. Young people carrying motivations that finally came to ground with devastating results, but ignored or not adequately questioned until the bodies were counted.

Law is the sure guiding element of society that keeps each of us in our own sphere of influence thus respecting those around us. To breach our rightful areas of influence is best described as trespass, going where we are not directed or allowed to go. Even in recent years we have seen what results when government is eroded and the way that man behaves in its absence. It appears that even Rousseau finally abandoned the hope of society for the individual learning on his own. But is the loss of governance an open invitation to illegality and evil. It has been said that locks are made to keep honest men honest. It is safe to say that laws with the power of the government keep most of us on the track to the good wishes for others. Although court cases are myriad with respect to issues of personal property and liability, the number of cases is relatively small compared to the numbers of potential deputes which could arise without due process. Such proceduralism does much to forestall more drastic actions on the part of those who consider their right to their own obstructive behavior. At times technicalities will result in a tragic miscarriage of justice, dismissal of charges which can reinforce lethal behaviors.

Violence is usually the result of having no recourse to arbitration and judgment in such matters. National enclaves may stand against others who would take their land and property under threat of death. But when man, in the security of his own domain, erects laws that tend to disallow the rights or others, and violence becomes the way of settling disputes of ownership, there is, under such circumstances of unilateral laws and rules, little suitable dispensation for all involved. When those charged with the responsibility of adhering to the law appoint others to work the law to the leadership's advantage, the democracy has fallen. A nation recognizes its right to exist and to provide for all members. If taking from another person, group or nation is the way that survival may be insured, then the law of confiscation may be appropriate to the needs of some, while not acceptable to the nation that lost its sovereignty and for those that may have been killed in the theft. Within an international community, do we need laws to cross borders? Do honest people need restraints; do we, in fact, need laws that respect others?

Need for Law

John Dewey's pragmatism has proven a widely held and pivotal understanding in the years since his active pronouncements of uncertainty and individualism of experimental authority. As America's foremost philosopher if he had lived on the Continent, it has been said, he could have been the father of both existentialism and postmodernism. His influence during his lifetime (1859-1952) was not so influential philosophically during his lifetime but has made up for its obscurity since his death. His belief that life was to be guided by our individual experience and that we should feign exclusive value in essentialism, made him a philosophical influence as worthy as that of Sartre or Camus. His belief in the uncertain nature of life could have given him the immediate authorship of postmodernism rather than Foucault or Derrida. Dewey' philosophy during his lifetime did catch on in the academy and his ideas have never fully left education of the public schools in America. His pragmatism, now seen as an general American philosophy has come to settled, in more modern times, into our culture.

It is often said that pragmatism is merely identifying and acting on what works, unfortunately this can still be applied if one decides to overlook the law. If you were to ask someone for an opinion only to find that it differed from yours, yet the other person was perfectly willing to concede your opinion to you, you are seeing the work of Dewey's individual authority and the implications of uncertainty in what should be reasoned obvious contradiction. If this tendency can be extended to every issue, to issues of law, in particular, then the strength of societal bonds are decisively weakened. This is of course contrary to Dewey's view that the seat of ultimate authority should be community and not the individual, to whom he gave immediate authority. His ideas of uncertainty and experience have, for many, become the filters through which we sample life. We are allowed great latitude in our personal lives in these modern or postmodern times far beyond the ancient laws that stood against spitting on the sidewalk or showing one's legs in public, but what are the limits to which we will exceed our system of laws?

Modern View of Law and its Value

We have abnegated our duty to children and in some cases to the elderly, changing laws as needed to meet the need of an activist citizenry. Law has become for many activists, merely suggestions possibly fraught with outcomes undesirable to them. Law as a guiding objective understanding of how we must entertain the needs of others has become a way to justify one's own needs in the misleading attempt to highlight others in their issues of personal plight. Yet the laws that intercede for citizens held close to the needs of individuals in finding rights and privileges, have become mutable although mankind has not changed. Rights have become broadly interpreted for the benefit of those who would have their specifically claimed rights inculcated into the law, while other at the same time have their rights impugned as a result. Because we have changed our understanding of law does not mean that our laws should be changed without full consideration of our systematic understanding of law, which now by law must be given room for the addition of lesser mandates which may run counter to those so long established. We are in a game where the out of bounds line is being changed by the players without an official alignment which would in the long run favor the visiting team. Abortion law has made euthanasia of the elderly possible, and general and ubiquitous legalized suicide may be next. Any laws added to the system must be studied for their possible consequences and erosion of the authority of old laws by the new.

Chapter 2

Leadership

Changes in the Law

Like the Segestans we have by will or by unmindful attrition of values given our laws and mores away to incursive influences. Most laws are written and enacted to guard against the erosion of constancy needed for the protection of all people. When that erosion is allowed even promoted, it usually starts with community and national leaders that lead the attack. Some laws that prove unjust have had detractors from their inception. Slavery is one of the most egregious examples, but due to an insufficient will of the people and the workings of extra-legal forces, prohibition was found to be unworkable while slavery's abolition has become a salient mark of a well-informed and sensitive, cultured society today for all blacks in our country as it should   have been always. It was not based on, or should not have been based on, the emotive forces working to outlaw slavery but the intent of the law's provisions for laws that guarantee equality and fairness. Yet the seeming unworkable nature of laws found to be insufficient for feelings must not always be allowed to determine whether that law is allowed to stand or is rescinded by the vote of the people. Law does not stand as a isolated prohibition but often a vital part of a system of protections for which leaders cannot always determine the extended effect of changing laws. Original provisions for abortion laws provided initially that incest and rape was a justifiable reason for an abortion, but that seemed to move beyond its original purpose to allow abortions for any reason and at any time before birth. With tens of millions of American babies having been aborted we find ourselves pushing the envelope for the normal expansion of the work force and possibly with time and the continued abortive inclination within our land, so the possibility of the right-to-die at any time for any reason may be enacted.

The leadership required to accomplish repeal must be well organized and determined to meet the requirements for negating not only the law but any preference for the law to stand. The question must be asked in each case as a general rule whether repeal or retention of the voluntary taking of individual life would, in the long run, serve the people, and whether the ultimate decision about the law should not be to handle a legal problem by changing or reaffirming a law which has a finite window of importance in terms of the vast system of laws. Should the law merely reflect the solution to problems that are inappropriately established within society, as convenience, or which has only limited importance for the behavior of a small segment of the whole of society.

Laws should be passed and supported by obedience to them. Laws which have broad community-favorable support and not a limited appeal to a part of the population seeking a temporal or individual solution should be protested until appeal is granted. All laws of fairness should stand on their universality in favorable support of all the responsible community. Should all babies be aborted or only some. Perhaps abortion rights should be seen in the context of the whole of society and not that exclusively of a mother or father not wishing the responsibility of a child. With the rise in childless parents seeking children through adoption, these laws tend to provide an immediate solution for the mother while other parents await an opportunity to adopt children. Society could profit from the living contributions of children unwanted by their parents.

If a baby is aborted is it different from the baby that is wanted, that grows to maturity and votes acknowledging his or her valid membership in the country of laws. This raises questions about laws that can be rolled out as needed. Laws that are controversial are usually those that seem to have gone by the way in acceptance and offer little significance or acceptance by the people as a whole. When laws are not repealed but linger and are relied on as singular examples of laws outdated or no longer pertinent these are not appropriate to any discussion or should not be put forth in legal discussion for the timely promotion of special interest legislation.

Furthermore, any tendency to bend the law to have emotivist inclusion of any particular consideration of rights may see law become, as it is sometimes now seem in some cases, a matter of feelings and not based on legality. Law may become little more than the justification for personal acts and ideologies. In the case of the common will, a majority of voters must establish the general acceptability of a law. Minority appeals may appear to justify legal action, but the smaller the inroad into the minds and hearts of a people, the less significant that law may prove over time as those that invoked their will to enact the law will stand for the law as its appeal to the majority wanes. Laws that out stay their welcome become a crippling legality in our system of laws, and laws that change the minds and hearts of the citizens because they have won the war of attrition need to be reexamined in an ongoing dialog of preferences and .

Elected and Appointed Leaders

Those government officials that are permitted to change laws hold their office in a sacred trust to serve the people they represent. To pass laws, a legislature should have the general support of both bodies of Congress. To do less, to write party or executive law is to misrepresent a sizable element of society which is more faithfully represented by the Congress and pushes through without compromise a law that does not support the whole will of the people, and is unjust. Laws must have the weight not of majority but of a national holism of support from pole to pole, far left to far right. If this does not happen, and the legislative branch is compromised in its addenda, then the law will become a divisive barrier to cooperation in other legislative matters. Whether one agrees with the provisions of the law, it is a singularly partisan package of mandates when only one party exclusively votes for the law and another does not. There is no wonder that the majority of voters have found disfavor with such laws even as the objection is worn away over time to a neutrality or a mind numbing malaise resulting in passive acceptance. But a stalemate of the houses of the legislature prevent any tweaking or compromise in the law. Not to allow legislative changes or modifications in the law's provisions by the legislature, a tendency promoted by both parties, is undemocratic andpossibly a one-sided legality.

If the president uses his executive power to write law even when the Congress has exclusive rights to regulate and pass laws, he thus becomes the legislature. When enforcement officers like attorney generals have concluded that they may bypass the will of the people recorded in votes and not enforce certain laws on which voters have clearly spoken but to set that vote aside and make a decision for themselves, then democratic enforcement of law has been breached. This is the thinking of Democratic ideologues, but such has also been the case with Republican leaders at times. Our leaders are elected to preserve the dignity of law, and write law and not fail to enforce laws because they do not like them or acquiesce to an ideological base.

Apathy and Leadership

Ideologues in government are those that do not have the authoritative concerns of the American people at heart. Somehow the lifelong pursuit of a career in the government leaves these people, for the most part, cynical and uncaring. It would seem that in government familiarity breeds contempt. For the so-called civil servants are hardly servants of the people, since they make more money and have better benefits on average than their non-public counterparts and can demand the compliance of citizens to their will and wishes under penalty of law. Along with the disinterest in preserving and adhering to the laws, the attitude of self-importance of this aristocratic rule is unacceptable. This is exactly where my two friends and myself in our discussion converge. This is unacceptable and cannot be allowed to continue. One of my friend suggested that Jefferson would support an overthrow while my other friend felt that a more basic yet peaceful transition to real individual representation should be commenced. My understanding reflects the general and pervading contempt that many Americans have for the least of laws, who elect improper representatives of the law, and who bear the responsibility for a failed leadership.

Chapter 3

Laws and Cultural Impact

Laws and Overregulation

Cynicism has been defined as an attitude of self-importance and self-promotion. This view easily accommodates exclusive knowledge or ability and in government it becomes the negation of concern for the people who should be represented. This malpractice has manifest itself in the "service" of the electorate from the IRS to the VA scandal. When the servant mandate is not observed then the oligarchs define their jobs for their own benefits with favorable job evaluations and bonuses. An overregulation by the government amounts to redirecting laws that are favored by administrative ideologues by giving an extremist tweak so as to change the law's original purpose through overemphasizing the law or provisions in the law such that the original intent is often overshadowed or lost. Treasury and energy departments ramp up regulations to the disadvantage of their country's citizens. This piling on of regulations beyond an ability to provide help to the citizens is a blatant move toward non-democratic oligarchy. If laws are redefined by regulation and emphasis of those features of properly passed laws that unbalance provisions within the law, then the laws are de facto new laws enacted by illegal legislation arrived at by bureaucratic fiat.

Victimless Crime

The idea of victimless crimes is often touted as a defense of not just a smaller governance but a smaller government with fewer laws while retaining laws that do not invalidate the privacy of citizens. The defense breaks down in most fleshed out examples: narcotic access, national defense and deregulation of all business law. In general the idea of more freedom and less government intrusion into the lives of its citizens is the short answer when ask what libertarians believe. This rapidly growing political party affiliation believes in balancing budgets but this alone is not enough to seamlessly join them to other conservative ideas. For instance legalizing drugs is not a conservative idea despite the fact that it would save enforcement costs such as police time. In fact this is far more liberal a concept than most liberals would support. Because libertarians do not believe that the government should pay for abortion, many still would allow abortions to be had by those who want them. The decision still holds that the individual may still seek an abortion, however, it should not be paid for by the government. This political philosophy is infusing itself into the conservative wing of the political dichotomy by stressing a balanced budget, while holding personal rights beliefs that even challenge more liberal democratic politicians. The effect is to take a dimmer view of law and lawfulness to the extent that the loss of respect for law through such variance from present law is arising in the mind of more and more citizens. Many young people have gravitated toward libertarianism thinking that since they may have adopted a simpler lifestyle than say their parents, simpler government with fewer laws yet with a balanced governmental budget, just like their personal budgets, should be required.

The overall effect of legal inconsistencies and abuses is that legal disregard and frivolous laws are bringing the value of law into doubt. Doubting the law abrades a respect for all citizens. To allow an adult or a child to legally acquire drugs in the absence of laws to protect from addiction and death results in the loss of laws without consideration of the interrelationship between citizens being able to do as they wish toward their own destructive tendencies. The very collective reasoning for the laws is thus scarified in collective sense. To take the criminality out of drug dealing may remove the threat that someone may be killed by drug dealers, but allows the non-victims, so called, to kill themselves by a method for which the addicted victim has little recourse on his or her own to stop. This approach to reducing drug dealing will only allow emphasis to be channeled to some new underworld moneymaker by the pushers and cartels. Criminals will always find ways to make money at the expense of others. Can we get rid of most laws or fail to pass laws that can protect citizens from the criminal element? Ultimately citizens will move away from the concern for others for the concern that intrusive laws are unfair, leaving citizens to be left to even unhealthy and unprotected activities; a particular problem when children are concerned. Minds addled by drugs do not think of others only their own hedonistic thrills or addiction, so we must protect them.

Isolation and Technology

Legal coalitions have the effect of causing people to interact out of support or opposition to laws. Laws can be changed, with difficulty, but serve as a fabric of restraint for communal activities. Protecting and organizing our efforts around communal laws promotes specific organizational plans. Good laws promote communal stability while bad laws, and there are bad laws, interfere with smooth public interaction.

But there is another factor, new to our world, that is further disrupting necessary community. Much of what passes for social interaction is really data transfers. This substitution for real world encounters may begin to appear as if it were equivalent to community and cultural interaction. When a high school student body decided that they would rather not have a prom but instead stay home and text friends, the fabric of community that hold a people together in face to face encounters, is beginning to show worn threads. The idea of friendship is becoming digital. Without facing another, one person can friend or unfriend another by simply texting or clicking a button on a website. There is the threat that the impersonality that gives us communication by data transfers which are less likely to effectively communicate a flesh and blood exchange of information with feeling and humanity, may be a gateway to mass killings in which people are merely obstacles in the way of the shooter's will.

Monocracy

If and when the isolationism by technology and a broader disrespect for laws settles in, can we expect that the adherence to this boarder neglect may bring protective laws into disrepute? Everyone deciding what laws are good laws and what laws are bad laws, which should be obeyed and which denied respectful adherence, does not bode well for the future of democracy. The choice about law's value, therefore, the value of the other people and their right to be protected by the government is the issue here. Make no mistake about it. When we pick and choose laws to obey and those to ignore and disobey, we have become a monocratic element of democratic dissolution. Chaos reigns when good men do what they want without the concern for the well-being of others.

Minocracy

What if all the minority groups bound together to work toward a collective rule which would would dominate the majority will? This has and does occur when the monocratic elements of society, those that have only their concerns at heart, unite their egotistic desire, often for overrepresentation in the law, to tactically take down the majority rule and the system of laws. A minocracy, as it is called, would miss the goal of a truly democratic representative system of law for all citizens raising the express will of minorities over that of the majority. This is the direction in which law is heading. Laws which answer the supposed needs of the minority, apart from the laws that bring the minority into the majority frame guaranteeing the same rights and integrating them into the system of work and reward, are to strain justice in the practice of civil law in the next few decades. Even now we are letting court precedent append and, de facto, amend our system of common law to give advantage to special cases, those which have been deemed by their own estimation and that of court decisions to be undeniable rights. The status of authoritative law is beginning to fall under the weight of modification and truncation giving law over to the assemblage of an admixture of laws. Once permanent and enduring laws which were held so long for the protection of all citizens are without adequate testing possibly compromising and affecting the integrity of the nation's system of laws. The possibility and extent of success in this move to deal in specifically directed law will continue to provide the legal precedent for new rights claims.

Theocracy

There are nations that have state religions like England, but religion is separate from the law-making branch of the government. A nation that is ruled by the authority of religion is an iffy proposition and very possibly is not a workable system on this earth. The breadth of religious paths to government are just as dicy as those from totalitarian to representative democracy. Since

God would not be in the flesh to rule, the religious leaders would make decisions and establish rules. This is particularly significant, since when Jesus preached it was at times against the very religious leadership of the Jews. They not only had turned religion into a simplified to-do list but had turned on Jesus with deadly intentions. This is hardly the tolerance that we have generally come to believe is the modern understanding of a responsible religious leadership. The leadership of a theocracy would not be necessarily doing God's work but taking spiritual convictions and trying to turn them into lawful decrees, without the direct sanctions of God. And we do have an example of an immoderate if not atavistic and despotic theocracy bent on establishing a world-wide caliphate. Radical Islam is the latest and most intolerant of religious freedom and worship in our time.

Other Forms of Rule

The number of possible governmental rules is staggering. Whether it is some variety of meritocracy, an ethnic rule (ethnocracy), or a rule that depends on knowing something, ostensibly what needs to be known to govern (epistemocracy). Or a demarchy, the random selection of ruling citizens, or even a kleptocracy in which the government is run by the wealthy and powerful or by a monarchy which sees government's role as protectively limited for the benefit of its citizens. These and all forms of government or the archaistic opposition to forms of government propose to be what in fact they probably will never be except the logocracy in which only words are given to government and not necessarily given to appropriate action. The latter seems to be what American's are suffering now. All talk and little progress, a word that should scare everyone only slightly less than that of structural tribalism in which the base is maintained relatively unchanged except for the enactment of ideological laws while little if anything is done generally for the citizens; the oligarchs rule apart from the courts, and the legislature protect their own concerns. Even as citizens die or languish in fixed and inferior lifestyles, the leadership only grades government's success by the maintenance of a functional membership and ideology despite the lost of individual members, who are not important if the purpose of the membership is not compromised. The structure of the government is all that is important.

Picking and Choosing

But Americans have a simpler approach to law. Take what you want and leave the rest. Do not consider others in your decision, just act as you will. It would seem that the citizen's preferred choice would be the panarchracy which would allow anyone to opt out of the authoritative enforcement of laws if the citizen so decides, while remaining within the jurisdictional location. This is not only anarchical but is selfish and non-democratic as well as destructive to the system of laws that have been laid in in a carefully interdependent holism by which all laws within the system are self-sustaining, democratic and sympathetic.

42

Laws and Jurisdictions

But if states decide to pick and chose or the Federal government decides to throw out laws that an administration finds outdated or ideologically undesirable, then the problem becomes much greater. One state can fail to enforce or ignore laws that may prove incommensurate with certain laws of other states. This could, and would with time, become the law of a state whose citizens did not endorse or vote for those laws. With such legal reciprocity passing laws which may unbalance the system of laws in one state could force acceptance in all other states overtime. This is not out of reason considering that laws that were the direct voice of the electorate vote have been put aside by the Department of Justice because they did not like the winning vote. This tabling of laws is the epitome of despotic oligarchs and totalitarian governmental practice.

Chapter 4

Law and Governance

Legal Interpretation

Law has a variety of meanings depending on the form of government in which it is given. In a totalitarian government, the law may be more interpretive to the extent that treason is merely the questioning of or the opposing of authority. As Russia is in the process of manipulating eastern Ukraine the importation of soldiers to disrupt and destabilize the Ukraine government is said to be not a military activity but the uprising of citizens. The justification is dependent however on the Ukrainians being still seen as a Russian enclave. The definition of citizenship is given by the ultimate intent of the Russian government, to take over a sovereign country for the national purposes of partially annexing a sovereign country into an abbreviated U.S.S.R now and a larger inclusion and representation of the old regime possibly in the future.

In a democratic society, the law is for the interpretation by those in power which depends often on disposition to particular laws. The Clinton Administration decided not to deftly pursue pornographic offenders, and when the White House was vacated by the Clintons and their staff a the end of their terms, the White House printers were said to harbor pornographic materials, lewd graffiti was found scrawled on walls, desks turned upside down and computer keyboards sabotaged and file cabinets glued shut. In light of these charges against the Clinton executive administration, which when these juvenile illegalities were carried out, there was obviously no executive policy to pursue these offenders. For the administration appeared to create an atmosphere favorable to such felonious interests. Computers were trashed, computer keys removed, especially the "W" keys which were stuck to the wall above doors. This was a childish but dangerous felony, since to interrupt the work of the White House is against the law. No one was arrested. No one was charged. If you must commit a crime, make it look childish, and commit a crime at the highest level of government, break laws too big and yet too infantile for you to be hauled in and charged.

Smaller government, which Republicans and Libertarians say they believe in, would go a long way to reduce the abuses of government by government, but an attempt to do this failed during Bush the younger's administration. When the president proposed that private charities take over some of the responsibility for the needy, it was presented in hope that it would result in a smaller government conceding to reduced control of the welfare system over those in need. It was opposed by the left who believe that government is the only answer. There were those who felt that charity in the hands of the public could bring condescension to the needy and back patting by the providers. Some felt that the government could avoid this self-serving altruistic public policy, grow the government in size and power to maintain a larger government providing for the needs of the disadvantaged, and opposed to private efforts.

When government authorities tell underlings that they do not have to enforce laws with which they do not agree, in particular laws opposing gay marriage, then the back of the system of laws has been broken. Handing down such an edict from high office is tantamount to appealing or writing law, an exclusive function of the legislature, and in effect negates the enforcement of law in the land. Is it any wonder that laws are broken without compunction day in and day out when our country's governmental leaders will not stand for the law, affirmed through the electorate. This picking and choosing gives Americans just one example that the idea of law is discretionary, that it literally does not bear the weight of the authority and is, therefore, to be interpreted by those who are sworn to enforce those laws. This is dereliction of duty and malpractice. The question must be asked whether anyone can so break the law. The answer seems to be yes in practice, for, if our leaders can do it, then as far as the law should be concerned, since a leader has no more right to avert law than any other citizen, any citizen would appear to have the right to deny any law's right to authority for which that that citizen does not claim favor.

Definition of Law

The law is the "binding" rules of a community or country in which the enforcement is mandatory for violators if the laws broken result in felonious and otherwise violations of law's authority. When government officials decide that some laws of the land are to be by passed merely on the whim of individual judgment, then the law has lost all authority and can be marginalized and subverted in any way. The law protects the progress within society guaranteeing that, as generally held, the protection of the citizens can be defended under penalty of prosecution and sentencing. The failure to enforce one law is the sacrificial destruction of the law as a body of interlacing protections. Not to be totally protected the citizen is left in the lurch with out due process and unable to defend a right position in front of a group of peers.

The law is a mirror for its citizens in a democracy. It represents the horizon in time and space beyond which we are unable to see. When we perfect the law and its enforcement for the issuing of opinions on the immediacy of legal consideration, we damage the process by which we are protected. Looking into a broken mirror gives only the distortion of the present and does not look to the future in expectation of laws protections and the past for historical relevance. Once the mirror is cracked, its fragmented reflection does not unite the parts that stand in reality, but the parts become the estimations of immediacy and need, ever ybroken piece is incapable of providing clear and holistic understanding.

Constitutional laws that are passed from the statutory resolve of government must be founded, not on a whim or some immediate societal avoidance or acceptance but must weave their way though the ratification process state by states in order to find ubiquitous authority. This was done to prevent anyone from picking and choosing what was desired and what was not desirable in writing laws. Our foundational protections were meant to provide a stable society which rested on these inalienable protections. The fact that modernity has given a new spin on society and what it would become has nothing to do with the enforceability of law given by congress or constitutional declaration. Laws are defined by the timeless content and the procedural protections insured in our founding.

Chapter 5

Law and Societal Mutualism

Societal Respect

One of the effects of the technological age is that we seem to believe that society can be bound together by text messages, phone conversations and Skype. We are loosing the intimacy and the honesty of face to face encounters, good or bad, the reassurance of favorable encounters and the stern face of rebuke. We have little to truly recommend us to potentially thousands of people that we might like or dislike on Facebook. It is hard to have concern for someone who amounts to little more than pixels on a hand-held device, and who we may not even have seen in the flesh. Respect does not come from data transfers but from the time spent enjoying each other in person, confronting one another with our differences and empathizing with those with whom we cry and laugh, feeling the tears, cathecting in sorrow and joy. How can we accomplish that intimate relationship without being truly part of our friends, our real friends, time of pain and pleasure. This interdependence of parties where we have mutual needs will be referred to here as mutualism, as a descriptor of societal bonds, including both citizens and the government.

The proper response to a friend's pain or joy is to experience through personal and present relationships the vacillation in mood and the timely need for sympathy or empathy. To know that a friend is suffering is not the same as holding that friendship in the flesh in a timely manner for establishing a growth in trust as a function of being there for a needy friend.

Government cannot offer the same repair and reparations for personal loss or trauma. The tribal and liberal approach is to carve out laws and regulations that do not consider the plight of the lowliest of citizen but set as goals provisions for the larger ideology and secondarily part of the citizen population. An ideological government is more likely to fulfill an objective than consider the plight of even the supporting electorate. Jobs lost from regulation, say, the improvement of the world's air quality, is said to only contribute about one percent in effect in world-wide pollution by greenhouse gases, therefore, this governmental intrusion into the wellbeing of theAmerican citizenry is virtually not in any substantial way significantly affecting the overall world pollution problem. Jobs and industry will be sacrificed to this ideology. Those on board with the policy have great ideological respect for the regulations but real people suffer without jobs for an insignificant change in world air quality and any possible climate change. Under the cover of ecological responsibility, loss of jobs and a general disregard for those who lose jobs points to the lack of social responsibility that is produced when all is granted to ideology. Furthermore, the supposed ecological constraints that prevent America from become independent of other country's energy supplies will be seen as major disconcertion of national need by an administration that would rather appeal to their green base than provide the energy cost reduction that business and citizens need and deserve to help maintain their prosperous lifestyles.

Mutualism and Law

The law when heeded should provide mutual protection both for the plaintiff and the defendant. Who is the injurer and who is the injured may be difficult to sort out, yet there is the concern that argument in court refereed by a judge and even at times a jury can determine this reinforced by the right to an appeal. And although judgments are the result of human activity, most citizens find justice in the courts, and the value of the court and a trial is equal protection under a system of laws. Are there miscarriages of justice? Of course judges and jurors are fallible. But there is recourse to find justice when either side in a trial believes that they have been poorly represented or that there is evidence that did not get heard or was not given attention at the time of the trial or preliminary hearing. Appeals may go on for years even decades, but mutual protection reaches out to all parties in the provisions made in the letter and system for which our countries democratic principles are made foundational.

Mutualism is the provision in the law that puts the burden of proof on both parties and the promise that each side will be given equality before the law both in public policy and in the courts. Does this become compromised when a judge or attorney circumvents the law for a position that is personal or political? When anyone associated with a law, enforcement of the law or any consideration of a law allows preference to intervene in its full and lively application, then the law is not compromised, it has been violated, broken by malpractice. Any alteration in the natural and effective application of the law must be seen as malpractice as there is no way to insure that all those on either side of the law will be adequately represented before the law. When the authorities stand on one side tipping the balance then the law has been circumvented and injustice has been done.

Social Implications of Unbalancing Mutualism

Legal interventionism can only disturb equilibrium in the delicate balancing of provisions to insure the rights of those bringing charges and those on trial. The effect on the social fabric cannot be always foreseen at the time that new laws are enacted. Law is an interlocking fortress against illegal procedure and holds all sides in check to the will of the law, justice. If the law is rightly divided, then justice more often will out in the beginning, if not, a new assessor of guilt or liability will be offered up in the form of new laws. To fail to impose the weight of law or to alter the intent and extent effected by new law designed to accomplish narrow justice may be to disrupt and unbalance the process by which justice is guaranteed and possibly the avoidance of other laws contingent on application of the new law.

When lawyers and courts negotiate pleas and sentencing times as if they were bidding for a sofa on ebay, arguing what will the state get and what will the felon get, leaves the citizenry out of the disposition of the case. This is not an appropriate ways to represent the law for the citizenry nor appropriate to the life of one who is convicted. The felon is given the best deal that can be negotiated with the advantage of years and months falling to the felon who, depending on the deal, may be less likely to be victimized in the process but more likely to be given a sentence that is unfair and minimal. This suggests that the law may be turned on the argumentation of a superior council or a zealous judge leading one to suggest that either side's case may be jeopardized by a better lawyer and a suggestible judge or poor counsel and an unfair judgement and sentencing.

Neo-legalism, seeing the law as a mutable force to realign the legal system with the over-weighted new laws compromising the system of law, is now changing the way that we supposedly see justice being reshaped. An understanding of the new direction of law is to not see as inalienable those laws among the holism of our legal justice system by which we have been served over two centuries, the law on which our freedoms and democratically organized government has been dependent.

Chapter 6

Law Enforcement

Hobbling the Law

When courts allow preference in law, other than the working out of the law in trial situations among peers with fair adjudication, then the law may be enforced unfairly. Prior to any court decision, the dispensation of the court creates a void of lawful application, a lawlessness for the police and arresting officers. When laws are allowed to flounder in the courts, the de facto feedback to the enforcement officers may be to alter their arrest criteria. If cannabis is given in small amounts to be only for personal use and there could be little good in arresting a user, then that shifts the overall emphasis on possession of any marijuana. Someone may avoid arrest for possession under special circumstance, like a first time possession at the discretion of the officers on the scene, or the standard arrest procedure may be shifted out of balance in order to negotiate a deal for turning state's evidence, which reaches for higher crime but in the process minimizes the the felony of possession. Over time drug possession may become a lever for accessing evidence for crimes that may result in injury and death, thus possession may become set aside as the weight of drug possession seems to be less an illegal infraction of the law than a law enforcement tool to capture more dangerous felons. At the level of enforcement of the laws against possession, the rules that balance the protection of the public and the rights of the incarcerated felon, must be balanced and the issues ultimately weighed in a fair and honest court trial. To do less is to violate the letter of the law, by which the law is seen to be in negotiation with itself.

Multiple Points of Discretion

It is unlawfulness to adjudicate with a dismissive attitude by preference or the negotiating of law. When combined these additive adjustments to laws and sentencing may result in a jury which cannot clearly determine the crime's impact on the victim and society, in the long run, based on the verdict and ruling by the judge. The extreme example is when a felon is turned out on the street when the case is dismissed on a technicality that prevents the evidence from being heard or weighed in judgment. Lawfulness, so called, becomes a tool with which violations of the law may be excused. Among the various options in the legal process whereby laws are negotiated, excused and disregarded, the citizenry is developing a callous disconcert for obedience to law.

Law is being bent and evaded by those who see it as a creative medium by which interpretation can streamline prosecution making a slow process doable with shorter lines for sentencing and incarceration. Likewise those in prison are being released for the added space made available by early paroles and commuting time. Yet another way in which the law is being marked down reweaving the fabric of this nation. If we were discussing personal budget here were would take the lack of resources as a sound reason for cutting spending, possibly a harsh measure, but necessarily a economic requirement to solvency. Our approach to overcrowded criminal courts and prisons is to catch and release in order to meet, what is seen as the lack of prisons and court time needed to process all those brought into the justice system, the message being sent that there is no room instead of increasing the jail time and making felony sentencing harsher to meet the less than adequate room for incarceration. The system must honestly work within a compromising and inadequate prison system by not cutting deals and serving up increased jail time in order to increase the number of inmates and decrease the appeal process which is excessive and unfair to both the public for time and expense and those locked up hoping for a judicial error to exonerate them.

Chapter 7

The Weight of Law

Perspective and the Law

How do we see the law and laws? If the laws can be bent and broken from the top down, how should we, the governed, see laws? Are they suggestions only to be ignored by courts and councils and so we may have the same dismissive attitude that we might see modeled for us? Without the benefit of legal knowledge can most of us rightly divide the laws that are essential and those that are negotiable, as if any laws were negotiable? Certainly we have no right to decide whether a murder is to be prosecuted or overlooked. What about crimes involving money, embezzlement and taking funds under false pretenses; can we make the decision based on our feelings as peers about whether the felon needed the money or that the robbery was the just deserts for those that steal from the rich?

What should be our perspective? If we were jurors should we find the robbers not guilty because we feel that the robbers could use the money more than greedy businessmen, who were really not victims. They had more money than they could ever use. Since they had more wealth than they needed, can we see the money as merely lost to a good cause and excuse the felons in the name of equalization of means and forgive the robbers by equivocation on the law and our own disregard for the law? We have had the anti-heroics of James Bond, for instance, breaking the law in the name of a government for at least six decades. If the bad guys are disposed of in the end, then the felonious acts committed in the process of their capture or killing is justified. If the highest authority sanctions the action then the process is protected. Robbin Hood could find mass support for stealing from the rich, as jurors may find for a defendant in a liability case to the disadvantage of a wealthy corporation, not based necessarily on the facts of the case but rather to the disparity of wealth which may be emotionally represented as illegal and immoral. When the government says that there needs to be a redistribution of the wealth, this has the force of government but only amounts to clearing the game board, starting over and reassigning the money equally to all players. The procedural mechanics of redistribution of wealth may obey game rules but to the real victim, the one who worked to make the money and loses it, this is no game.

Law and License

Where do governmental agents and individuals find the license to evade the laws or reinterpret them out of original contexts. When those laws were written for the protection of the public and given as an ernest hope to the law-abiding citizens who worked hard and obeyed the law, not arbitrarily but as the force of authority given by law, uncompromised and vigorously protected, they had the foundational weight of a nation on which to rest. When groups and individuals oppose laws for their own benifit, clearly the reason seems more often to be self-serving and mean in effect. Changing the law is permissible under the the authoritative action of the legislature, but, when it changes the country in which the system of laws has authority, it is less advisable and should be looked at more closely than the wants and needs of one person or a group. A bonafide law, that is an indiscriminate law, should protect everyone and not require passage for the sake of special interests, nor should laws that decide guilt and innocence be massaged by the bench based not necessarily on the jurors' verdict but appended or amended by the inclination of the judge by his own understanding of guilt or innocence, right or wrong. A judge can mollify the decision of a jury of peers by ultimately ruling in sentencing without seriously considering the intent of a jury's decision.

As we have seen over the last several decades the judicial arm of the government has become a quasi-lawmaking system. By activist judges bypassing the legislature for more personally held ideals than societally ubiquitous needs seems to convince us that the fabric of law is second to the impress of individual petitions for precedent. Under such orders laws are not only decided to be suitable for the canon but are given the conditions under which the law may have merit. This is marginally legislative in effect and can effect the application of the law and the extent of its jurisdiction. As previously argued, gay marriage laws intended to give legality to marriages in one state may ultimately prove detrimental to laws that do not provide for gay marriage in another state. This could be the intent of activists, to ultimately sweep all the states and if necessary one by one, but it is unfair to those who have not by vote issued acceptance or rejection of same-sex marriage in their state.

The issues that arise with non-voter approval may have far reaching effects. Since the law may also have effect on the insurance, inheritance and ownership laws in that state, the law may cause, as we have seen in more and more cities and states, financial stress on the ability of businesses and government to fund the extensions of the law through insurance advantages and retirement benefits. What the law sees as clear is anything but clear to employers who may find financial obligation to gay-married employees, however, it could become excessively expensive for the government and employers. When marriage of an employee brings in new insurance coverage and maternity leave for adoptive parents, the budgeting for unexpected perks that must be provided by employers may become excessive, far beyond the perks expected for the employee when first hired. The law in this case may give gay-choice license to make unaffordable commands on their employers generosity for perks which have probably, in a stable work force, been calculated to be affordable for those recognized as single and those with otherwise insured partners. But perks could be a burden on employers who hire heterosexual employees who later marry for as legal interpretations to the law permit variance from our understanding of the one man one woman marriage laws, could not one take as many wives of different sexes or even make the same relationship among people as animals. This may seem   unreasonably remote, but when rights, so called, become the negotiable force of law, then we may not see the future so clearly through our past of reason and laws narrow application.

Minor Violations and the Law

In the course of the discussion with my two friends, I asked why those at the top needed to be removed? One friend's answer was that they were untrustworthy and needed to be removed to protect the citizens of our country. Yet my point was that those people had been given a chance to vote for leadership and who secondarily those elected official would appoint to carry out governmental duties. Furthermore, since those people had been put in power by the pubic vote, it would be difficult to claim that the unlawful leadership does not represent us. To say that the electing vote was the result of the candidate holding to some secondary consideration of law and its enforcement does not abrogate our responsibility for the remaining campaign pledges to which we have no liking. Once in conversation with a lady I was told that she was going to vote for a candidate who believed that abortion rights should be the law of the land. Although she did not believe in abortion, she like the candidates other policies. The voter must assume the responsibility for all the policies and programs for which the elected candidate supports. We cannot arrogate unto ourselves exoneration for those accompanying policies with which we are not in favor. This could mean that in an election where platform positions are unwanted, then no candidate should get one's vote. Perhaps we should support a provision by which a candidate on the slate is also voted on by the various positions that he or she plans to support, those particular position should receive a no vote as well as a yes vote as well as the candidate. .

Many elected officials may entertain legislation which we cannot regard as worthy. Are these representatives dishonestly taking liberties with the law? Is this then a lie which should care a legal intervention against the candidate. I would submit that elected officials are serving us, the majority, faithfully in those issues and purposes to which we have entrusted them.

The shift in the discussion with my friends is to our culpability in the matter of governance. Are we not as the electorate responsible for the keeping those in office who do not carry out the law, those that unlawfully carry out the law and those who do not completely agree with our political and moral position. The claim that we cannot legislate morality is countered by the abundance of laws about marriage, divorce and murder. Therefore, votes on the basis of moral conscious are correctly considered when deciding on a candidate. Those that do not meet the social, political and moral criteria for an elected official should not be voted for no matter their agreement with one or two of our pet causes. We continue to vote them in and rarely do anything to remove them, when, as we see it, they break the law. Thus, in the overall election process we give those that do not deserve to hold office a chance to do harm to the office and the laws they are sworn to support.

The example that was given to my friends in discussion was that we have responsibility in our actions to keep the law as an everyday occurrence. When driving down the expressway doing the speed limit, ever car around me speeds past and every car behind me is closing on me and I alone am keeping the law. This does not make me feel righteous and so much law-abiding as it does make me think that there are few that have regard for the law in the smaller things.

Every other driver is breaking the law. So, in this case, they are actually not respecting all the laws but maybe just the "big" ones, like the laws protecting us from murder and robbery. I have been told in other parts of the country people obey the speed limits. Is that only true of my part of the country. Is this a regional infraction? Do we break the law everyday or is this just a preference for illegality that is shown in our state and those in other state take their experience in illegality in not honoring parking meter time limits or fail to replace car license plates on time?

We are our on purveyors of legality. No matter where we live we sort and select those statutes for which we may have a liking and ignore the rest. With regard to the the speeding example, we break laws that we think are impeding our progress. We take the law to literally impede our progress on the road, our success and our sense of individual goodness. I would contend that that is no more than those that we elect may do. So why do we get so concerned? In this sense we are electing those who may have a low-level of respect for the law much as we do.

Choosing Illegality

Why do we break the law so wantonly? Speeding is not the result of getting our wives to the hospital for a delivery, not in all, perhaps in only the rarest of cases. It is not because most people are late for work or have important appointments and must not be late. We break the speeding laws because we want to. We have passed that person in the red car that cut us off; we have beaten them. We can go as fast as that little sports car, they sure seem self-important, but we stopped that for now. We are a mess. Certainly one factor that motivates us to speed is that there are not obvious deterrents around. There are no cops to be seen. We don't care about the law, we merely do not want to be caught and fined, and without legal consequences we will drive as we please. The idea that deterrents do not reduce crime cannot be addressed in a nation where a murderer may get off or serve shorter time than corporate embezzlement. Laws seem to stand protected in Singapore where caning is quick and unmitigated.

Yet despite the law against speeding, we take it as a personal yoke that we must bear. We never seem to register the danger with which others may have to undergo do to our selfishness. There is never the thought that our inclination to trespass the law could result in someone being injured. Perhaps their is some sense that the unthinkable will not happen to us; we will not injure anyone and our vehicle will not be damaged, certainly we will not be hurt. In this state of mind, to us the laws against speeding seems to be little more than an imposition of another's will, the will or the law, on ours. We even play fast and loose with the law, when we are in pedestrian mode. Most of us will jaywalk when the light that will permit us to cross the road more safely is only a few feet from our chosen crossing point, but we are willing to put someone driving a car in harms way even as we may not acknowledge that something horrific could result from us illegally crossing the street even our possibly being hit by a car. Statistics of pedestrian deaths do not phase us. My city is in the top ten for pedestrian deaths, yet we continue to cross dangerous intersections without lights and put drivers in harms way to successfully avoid hurting the pedestrian. The mark that a driver-pedestrian mishap would leave on a driver are horrendous and would live in the driver's thoughts for a lifetime, yet we will do what we want anyway we want. At risk of death and destruction we still hold our respect for the law in abeyance until it is sanctioned by a higher court, ourselves, and, with deference to the philosopher Nietzsche, our "will to power. "

Despite the seriousness posed by speeding we do not care that anyone sees us break the "little" laws. Even with staggeringly high littering fines, we will throw something, anything out the window of the car unless we see littering as an immoral act and may still litter on occasion. We must get rid of a truck load of waste materials and we find an empty lot for its disposal, even if it is posted with do not dump signs. Why do we do this? We will probably not get caught, there are no police in sight, so its alright.

Law's Complicity

It would seem that we are impervious to the lesser violations of the law. It helps that the law enforcement is often lax and seems to avoid much of what it is there to prevent - those little violations. The fact that we can escape the long arm of the law in small matters of legality may drive us to test the limits of its authority. We may take this as an indication of uncaring or laziness on the part of the police but we are set in our ways having not been sufficiently penalized by fines and blotches on our driving records and the police have their hands full often with much more serious violations of the law. Perhaps this is not just a bottom up decision to prioritize those violations of more flagrant and serious nature while making speeding something that is handled when possible between felons. In some cities or states there is said to be a limit on the amount of revenue that may be garnered from motor vehicle violations. I was told by a policeman that although the departments will not acknowledge the quotas for handing out tickets and fines, that it is a guarded reality in vehicular ticketing that each officer must bring in so many tickets and so at the end of the month the focus turns to moving vehicular violations.

This in itself, if it is true, means that once an officer reaches that proscribed level of ticketing, that others speeding or running red lights may not be stopped, despite their violations, thus freeing the police to tend to those more serious illegalities.

Our Complicity

Much of the lack of concern for such laws may be seen in the dubious enforcement of the law and the lack of consequences, not being caught. It may be correctly seen to be of low priority compared to robberies and killings, but it helps to embed a paralegal understanding of what is permissible and what is not. When we opt to take a chance believing that we will not be caught in minor violations of the law, we in effect, in our own mind, fatigue the elasticity of laws that are designed to snap back on the perpetrator. We wear down the usefulness of the law, unable to hold its own, in effect, encouraging others to take advantage of the relatively unchallenged laws. I was told by a friend that his employer had a very large workforce and had for a very long time been paying people that did not exist as if they were on the payroll. It may have been passed from one generation of administrators to another but it happens, I am told, in both the private- and the public-sector workplace. Medicare and Social Security are sending out checks to people who have died, but the checks are still being cashed. My point is that once the inability or unwillingness to rein in felons who steal money is inculcated into practice, although illegally, it may become over time a failure of bureaucracy to acknowledge and expunge the practice. Such a low percentage of those that get checks illegally may be considered in the overall percentage of good checks not worth the hassle of being called out.

When we break, what we may consider, the small laws and get away with it, perhaps we are encourage citizens to step up to more ambitious misdemeanors or even accepting illegal monies from the government. The question is will a lawless people step up and take the next step, to felonious activities, as a condition of having been guilty of the violation of lesser laws? Does higher crime occur predicated on a history of lesser crimes which serve as the gateway to felonies much as canabis has been said to be a gateway drug for more dangerous drugs. It could be argued that depending on the likelihood that one's illegalities may not be noticed or pursued, the citizen, law-abiding in the large areas of crime, may push the envelop and make forays into a life of calculated felonious violations.

Chapter 8

The Future of a Lawless People

The Will to Power

A German philosopher of the nineteenth century, Nietzsche, who was referred to in the last chapter, developed a philosophy of personal disinterest for others with an eye to the superior nature of self over others. He held that man was either a master or a slave. The power with which we lived our lives to establish ourselves as masters was a driving force in the establishment of a dominant persona and collectively, on a national scale, a successful state. Much of this rhetoric was echoed by Ayn Rand in objectivist philosophy who believed, or at least taught, that looking out for oneself and keeping all focus on self as an objective entity would allow others to be given their right to their own objective understanding and existence and by avoiding interference with others we would empower others to their own freedom and happiness or servitude.

Solipsism

It would seem that we are Nietzschean or even objectivist, with regard to the law, not to mention pragmatic, i. e. what ever works. These philosophies suffer from a denial that we have to have concern for others without our selfish natures giving only guidance to ourselves for our own success. Some have gotten very close to the denial that others even exist for us. This seems to be arising in the culture. While gaining influence by the passive acquisition of friends and acquaintances through social media, we can meet befriend and unfriend someone without ever seeing or talking to them in person. Exposing the most intimate details of ones life with what amounts to digital strangers is not intimacy at all, but the illusion of intimacy, a sort of digital voyeurism. The effect is to estrange people from another and give them a very impersonal view of relationships and caring for others as if others were actually not living and breathing humans.

If we can disregard our fellow man, even the laws that regulate relationships among us, our laws that provide mutual protection may be seen more so as suggestions while enforcement may seem more remote and unconcerned. As citizens begin to pick and choose laws to break not addressing the protective function of laws and disregarding the harm that may befall others as a result, we begin to venture into the realm of higher-level lawlessness. And when we add in the violation of law at higher levels, both in the criminal occurrences of crime and the governmental avoidance of laws passed to protect the citizenry, is there no wonder that the commitment to respecting law is in jeopardy. When we consider only ourselves and not others we are seeing the loss of community and, in effect, de facto, a denial that others exist.

Solitary Existence

As a united people under democratic rule it is destructive to our nation for citizens to isolate and segregate by solitary existence. We may have some disturbed citizens who crawl off into the woods to live away from others, but we need one another for if everyone would follow individual needs and wants only our country would be unable to defend our collective culture and our nation. If we think only of ourselves, an inclination that seems to be spreading, we run the risk of becoming a Segesta, void of true community, culture and law, unwilling to commit to our culture and ultimately giving our country and its culture away.

Solitude is enshrined in the lack of respect that comes from not communing with neighbors. Those that live near may be considered destructive to us and enemies of our lifestyle. Demographics are increasingly unable to practically represent groups formed in common interests and individuals choose to shun community for self. We are in effect compromising the protection of our communities and our nation. We are losing the very grounding that law requires to affect its purpose, to arbitrate differences and disadvantages. Given the more powerful advantage without adjudication by judicial referees sworn to uphold the law for both the powerful and needy, the government or an oligarchy becomes the master and the citizens the slaves. Since lawless people are often drawn to the disaffected in the population, a lack of law and adherence to the law brings about change promulgating illegal behaviors throughout communities especially in less integrated groups and individuals. Extrapolated to the extreme, those that live alone and act alone may become a law unto themselves and the community around becomes less than law abiding. Not only does community bind us together to a common good, but our behavior, indeed, our lawlessness would become more difficult to hide and individual accountability would necessarily increase.

My wife and I owned acreage in a rural and mountainous area and traveled over two hours to spend a day or so on the land. It was gorgeous. There were wildflowers and limestone bottom creeks that ran year round. This wonderland was isolated and sparsely populated, and because of its isolation this area grew most of the cannabis grown in the state. You could not be sure that you were not going to succumb to a grower's booby trap to guard the cannabis crops. There were neighbors that kept to themselves in defense of their property and livestock. Because many residence could not keep people off of their land without livestock and properties being vandalized, a local law was passed citing that to be on another citizen's property one needed a note of permission from the owner. This provision, of course, depended critically on the police being able to get to isolated farms and homes in time to protect the land owners. This kind of law among disparate citizens in isolated surrounding miles from any law enforcement was to be proved virtually useless.

The leaders and government members in this area had their finger on the pulse of all property owners.

They knew who they were and their work schedules allowing the powerful to surreptitiously remark property boundaries in the absence of the owner especially if they were known to live elsewhere only rarely visiting their property, and, when the property was sold, the sellers would realize less acreage and prime timber and farm land. The county records were changed and as the property, like much rural property today, cycled through owner after owner. The thefts were protected by multiple deeds and the passage of time.

All of this is to say that due to the sparse population, the small law enforcement local office and the general self-dependence on one's own wiles to make a living in an economically depressed area, there were hermits and criminals who took advantage to steal and harass for their own profit. The police were miles away from most rural homes and the residence became more self-reliant on their own defense of the land, a fact that resident criminals realized all too well. And in most cases the police were rarely able to defend citizens and ineffective in defending citizens in legal scrapes among powerful land owners and clever governmentally connected criminals.

Isolation bred in these people, possibly the lawlessness that grew up in these rural survivalists, maybe the result of necessity and a sort of individualized law by pre-intent, was made and had authority with the land owner. Law was an abstraction for most residents. Law was pragmatic, individual and absolute. This is what isolation can induce - in law that is blind to the real needs of the citizenry. The seriousness went well beyond property rights but extended to the right to life itself as some property owners in a similarly isolated area were actually killed. A neighbor told me that a military man who had served several tours in Vietnam had been killed on his own land. Law cannot be disentangled or shelved because it does not seem to work perfectly or represent some among the many. The result is the generation of perfunctory law-keeping that serves the purpose of the few at the expense of the majority without question even as the elderly and helpless unborn are in effect put out on the ice floe.

Chapter 9

Civil Society

Master and Slave

Law is the structural foundation for civil society. The outcome of groups not giving honor to law and its fair maintenance is the tendency to Nietzschean associations. Either master or slave was Nietzsche's understanding of relationships within groups. There was no charity, no help for others, because aiding someone to climb out of the slave category was to threaten one's on position as master. This meant less autonomy for those who did not have to completely answer to ethics and law. No one would be helped because the slave is seen as nothing more than an object. This had grave consequences in the hands of Hitler. Millions of deaths point up the extreme effects of such thinking: the veritable inability of community to exist among all people and the mastering of individuals by sacrificing societal bonding and cooperation, and as in the wilderness areas of America, people are disregarded as important and it is everyone for himself or herself.

Organic Predisposition and Society

Another detraction from the societal goal of cooperation and fair dealing, the foundation of law, comes from Daniel Dennett who sees all tasks perfunctory or complex as the work of a data driven brain which is hard and soft wired, but the brain is predetermine in many ways. There is no free will to direct actions to good, to bad, to law or to lawlessness for we have not complete control over the mind. It is an easily justifiable answer to the difference in those that adhere to the law and those that do not. It can, based on Dennett's ideas, justify all behavior good or bad as innate predisposition. Although the law is not what Dennett had immediately in mind, behavior becomes a self-fulfilling narrative where nurture is of dubious advantage and behavior is merely the result of the brain's neurological wiring. To think that some will invariably find lawless activities in which to prosper leaves the law without complete capacious merit. Law narrows and becomes rife for the manipulative direction for even those, in Dennett's estimation, who may not be genetically bent to crime and wrongdoing. But who is to say who is predetermined and who is not. If there are genes or epigenetic factors that dispose one to crime or anti-cultural behavior, then who could find justification for rendering judgment on such people. To go a step farther, are we not responsible for the deviation from the mean? Are we not all responsible by our influence? For that matter, who could claim guilt for one without claiming by communal influence that the guilt would have to be spread over the predispositions of many from the directing community. For by Dewey's reasoning we can never remove ourselves from blame for the acts of others because we are necessarily complicitous in their deeds.

Idealism and Learning the Law

The roots of idealism are found in the tenderness of the human spirit yet feelings re misplaced in legal decisions where the vexations of maintaining the law against the illusory inclinations to compromise the law through exceptions which are seen as the right way to a gentler and more sympathetic interpretation. Standing on the formality of law only, permits someone suspected of a crime to bypass the judgment of peers. When the merits of a case are bypassed on a technicality, the law is not served, and may also establish precedent influencing other cases that may follow. The law at times serves as a detention or temporary holding room where lawyers and judges roll up their sleeves and rummage around for the laws they like and those little technicalities that can be thrown into the mix of justice and crime to avoid or ameliorate judgment.

When cases are pleaded or negotiated this also robs victims of their rights. This may be done pragmatically for there is only so much jail space for offenders so the sentencing may be abbreviated and some cases that would stand for serious consequences may be plead down severely. Although it is not currently fashionable to broadcast the shear numbers of felonies unpunished in this way, if we were to hold to the rule of law and not just the procedural methodology, we might find that the number of criminals needing incarceration might tend lower overtime and their accommodations behind bars less crowded.

Finally, one approach seems to have its roots in idealistic understanding but makes assumptions that even go far beyond law's experience and trumps reason. The idea that has been at the forefront of sentencing and even the practice of education of the young is that if one knows one will do. This is the most egregious act of thoughtlessness to the victims of crime and a boon to the career criminal that has been perpetrated on America. It has its most sensitive impact on the young who take forgiveness for license as they begin their forays into a life of crime and are spurred on by a failure to make the law's verdicts disincentivize criminal activity. The obvious denial of such reasoning is that if knowing that you might get caught is not learned over felonies many times repeated, then knowing cannot produce law abiding citizens.   This ideas has been defeated based on the casuistry that doing   wrong   cannot   be   prevented   by   heavy punishment and taking life. It, I contend, has not been tried, for the reduced penalties of a soft-hearted jury and penal system. So give criminals a reason to not go into lifelong career crime, and don't compromise the law with procedural errors or technicalities preventing a criminal, in the face of overpowering evidence, to escape appropriate incarceration.

Without law, without the instinctive care of others man could have not flourished and populated the earth. The species would have become decimated and the rule of law, if it existed in any meaningful sense, would   have   become   a   nightmare,   a   Nietzschean nightmare. Civility and governmental authority is the only insulator between citizens and an aggressive criminal element whether found in the general community or in the government itself. Man cannot be given a pass in crime on the basis that we are contributory to felonious acts in our community nor that some will, despite our best efforts, will always break the law because of their disposition to illegal behavior. The only way to maintain a civil society is to punish those that commit criminal activities repeatedly by permanently or indefinitely separating them from society.

Chapter 10

Collapse of Culture
and Society

Fall of America

Over the last half of the previous century the imminent fall of America was predicated based on the takeover of our government. Although this may be the ultimate and final stage, the fall of America, if it happens, may more probably be the result of internal insipidity reminiscent of that of Segesta. Like the Segestans we are betraying the very foundations of our republic, the respect for laws and thereby the respect for other citizens. The Segestans were willing to be taken into Athens protective power, lose their culture and their laws to the Greeks. They sold their city. We are selling our legacy as we compromise the rule of law. Leaders and citizens do not respect the law but choosing those particular laws that they believe should not be violated and those that they do not care about or recognize, they break them selectively, it seems, at will. This is destructive to the fabric of democracy and laws that provide equal protection under the system of laws. Simply by allowing the law to suffer from a lack of respect and a failure to support it respectfully we may see the dissolution of our way of life opening up the doors to oppressive government which makes and over emphasizes laws as it needs to bolster its program of abusive governance. All freedom will be gone and protection of others will only be allowed if it serves the rulers purpose.

Violation of Civility

It is not the law, or the breaking of the law, that is in itself that which weakens modern American culture but the secondary effect of loss of mutual respect among its citizens. The law merely sets the parameters for lawful respect among the citizenry. Picking and choosing only emphasizes the points of friction for which differences concerning property and the freedom of daily activity may arise.

Reality television has become the new attitude adopted by many of our people. We may have little knowledge of the commitment that we must make to survive as a nation, yet we know the attitude that will assert our egos over those who we think might be challenging us and our rights. Polite communications and pardons face to face are virtually a thing of the past. We race our cars on the streets as if they were the engines for winning cash prizes conferred upon us as we arrive early at work. We cut people off in traffic and try not to be the only one that passes the careful driver going the speed limit. Our personality collectively, as a people, stinks. We are narcissistic, utilitarian and thankless. We are feckless in our mutual responsibilities to one another and unloving even to those that are often closest to us. The overall effect is one of cultural decay and dissolution of social graces.

These are the wreckers of society which displace the mutual respect of concerned citizens. In our actions we are willing to trade our republic to the whims of our lawlessness nature and our selfish desire to please ourselves without regard to the plight of others.

Maximalism

What is there to do with those that will not take a civil position and allow others the same rights that they would have? The law is definitely given for our protection of those people, but this is based on an assumption of a system of laws and the fair protection of all and not the passage of laws that protect a minority while compromising the majority. These people bent on their own laws do not seem to be able to live with equality but want their way despite the affect that the new laws will have on others. A Caring majority will find in everyday practice, a way to assure equality in all things. We must allow the minorities to find a lifestyle that does not take rights away from the majority and offer protection for them as all others have protection, and this is the best that can be done for them and should be done for them. To do more is to endanger the whole of society.

Return to Civility and the Law

"Your welcome" has been displaced by "no problem." "Excuse me" has fallen to mute intrusion and no apology for the minor violations of others. Our laws have been ameliorated by the fear that we might violate the feelings more than the rights of others. The result is a portion of the population that does not give to the health of a caring and involved public. Tennyson, the Victorian poet, captured this undeniable feeling in Ulysses: "...I mete and dole Unequal laws unto a savage race, That hoard, and sleep, and feed, and know not me." Things were not as they once were, which is America's fate also: for "We are not now that strength which in old days Moved earth and heaven; that which we are, we are..." We have lost our strength in unity. We seek for strength in our individual lives, as if each one of us on our own and owing nothing to anyone can manage the strength of the many. We have lost our sense of cultural unity, not as a result of the influx of people lawfully and unlawfully arrived, but by the loss of interdependency once gained by acceding and conceding to others. The reversal of which is the way back for our nation: to join as a nation and be willing to let others win when it is truly in the favor of both and more importantly in the favor of fairness and truth. To treat neighbors and citizens as equals who are as important as myself, even to elevate others above myself for the benefit of them and, for me, the attitudinal shift from self-preservation to my own reclamation through sacrifice and the charity of spirit.

Laws will then be respected, as they once were by most. People will share in the national bounty of freedom and self-respect as well as respect for others. Then once again we could be the pioneering people that gave all for unity of trust and truth and the belief that we do well when other do well.

Conclusion

When my friends and I were beginning our discussion about the government and its seeming lawlessness, I had no idea that the solution by which I would try and hold my own in the discussion would reflect the lawlessness of us all. This came as a shock to me, and raised the question, do I fit this lawless description? In the same time frame as the writing of this book, I had rediscovered a book which I had bought at a church parking lot book sale entitled, *Where the Road Divides*. Its secondary title was *Studies in Conduct with Character Case Conferences.* Stories were presented to allow students to sort out the right and wrong of situations while calling on the student readers to justify any understanding that they might have concerning the scenarios. The purpose was to present the student with enigmatic situations for which they were charged to find good understanding as if they were responsible for solving often complex inter-relational disputes as those that might arrive in their daily lives. The idea was to use the case studies to teach how one answered to problems with peers. The overriding issues were not of legality so much as questions of morality and fair play. It struck me that this maybe the way back. All of our tendencies to find answers begins with the question of what it will profit me. There is little concern for what my decision will mean to someone who is set at disadvantage because of my attitude and action. Our active input into solutions to problems that begins and ends with us is at the heart of our failure to see others in a respectful manner. The road divides when we become the sole arbiter of issues of morality and seemliness, finding the like minded and pressing our views advising law in the process.

It was said that John Kerry in his bid for the Presidency could not find a way to bind all the support he felt he should have found in the liberal block because he could not present a unifying rhetoric for all the splitter groups that held each particular cause even to the exclusion of others in the party. He lost the election, it has been said, because everyone wanted something different and it is hard to impossible to coalesce a myriad of disparate ideas of fairness into a coherent policy. Although a more postmodern rendering of coalescence by admixture might have served him better, and I do not know if this fragmentation of support was a cause of the failure of his bid for office, but it seems that this is the dilemma for which our bid for a sound nation in the new millennium may suffer. How do we pass laws, and laws that will be respected, when everyone want something for themselves, some legal provision, other than what has been passed for everyone. And can we know that laws replaced or added to the system of laws will not do harm to laws we do not wish to affect by the change. For example, do we know the effect of same sex marriage will have on the ancillary laws concerning benefits and liabilities for unions and the overall allowance for benefits granted by employers or the extended effects on tax revenues? And can we know long term the effects by extension in such additive laws on the consequences of laws in one state affecting laws in another state by legal reciprocity.

And what about the VA scandal. How can it be explained? It may be that some of the people that were in charge of helping veterans and yet brought about their deaths through bureaucratic waiting lists and the sacrosanct low measure of the governmental workday, chose to withhold services to critically ill patients, allowing some to die, may not have broken the speed limit as an entry level misdemeanor to murder, but something changed. It is not too bold to say that what did change was commensurate with a loss of humanity, the loss of concern for others as they hid behind the bureaucratic framework in which services were to be rendered. And although there was no law that demanded that patients be seen with the immediacy of concern, the human response was quelled by inattention and selfishness. The system, however, gave opportunity to ignore the needy by the slow to start and quick to finish days and work weeks. A friend that had worked in a government lab told me that the work week was a joke, slow to begin and quick to finish early each week. Unions must carry some blame also as they maintained limits on work times and the protection of all not based on merit but on maximizing payment of union dues. The violation of the law in spirit must have happened long before the insensitivity to others. And if Dennett is right then how did all of these felons, not hired by nature, become involved in administrative malpractice suborning murder. Dispositional defense does not seem to justify or explain the calculated insensitivity of so many in so many parts of the country. This mass propensity to murder must therefore be the capability and capacity of us all. We need the laws to keep us honest and lawful, to give us the care of others under penalty of law.

Fiddling with the law adding to or selectively reconfiguring the law could have serious and adverse results. Do we begin our rebellion at the top of laws hierarchy or do we begin by a loss of respect for laws in general as our attitudes reduce all legal requirements to suggestions and then to proceed on with a now reimagined world in which our legal concerns and prospective laws become the interpretive rosetta stone for all others? The question then is raised, if this is understood correctly, and new laws become precedent for new law patterns and interpretation suggesting and pushing for our own laws of selfish intent. The pressures of private interests that do not concern themselves with the whole of society may produce disequilibrium among systematic laws as new laws are past that target only a small segment of the population.

Is it not time for all Americans to see to the upholding of all laws before we unbalance the system of laws that equilibrates ideas and needs with wants and that do not reflect the greater need? Is this not the greatest charitable donation that we can give to others and ourselves: that we uphold the rights of all first, and not the erosion of the rights of others. The democracy we enjoy was not arrived at in a vacuum but in a struggle for fairness and unity among laws in order to provide the broadest coverage of protection. To introduce individually inserted new laws into a holism of generally protective understandings denies the difficulty with which our system of law was carefully constructed and our resultant core values embraced. We must carefully consider the long term effect that substitutionary as well as additive laws will have on the overall clarity and justice of our systematic legal system.

And so my answer to my friends is that we cannot breach the system of law, which is all that we have to protect us and others against the mollification of law and hence the rule of the strong. To my friend who would tear down the government and rebuild, I would say that the history of such projects over time and around the world has not had such a good record. The Bolsheviks, Stalinists, Hitler's Aryans, Castro's Cuba and now the Caliphate willed by ISIS and looking at the Arab world as their own, have a record of atrocities. The rebuild would be our undoing with every faction wanting more than they could reasonably have.

To my friend who believed that we could possibly give the individual the nod to be foundational to our democracy, the reference to the despots of history tells us that we cannot decentralize authority to empower the One, for protection and accountability cannot be arranged except where we all adhere to a common system of laws, a representative democracy by which all citizens can and should be cared for and protected.

The change that could bring us to the epiphany of the value and protection offered by our system of laws can only come when we become the answer and not the problem. To change our lives to that of respecters of the law in all its facets and vagaries, to uphold all laws, to rejoice in the limits placed on us as they are the limits for us all and to think of law as a broad umbrella of protection for all and not just for some. To think that special laws more than highlight the need for protection for some and which may become the nucleus for parametric laws growing around such initial legislation may also be the beginning of usurpation of the holism of our system of laws developed around the wisdom of our founders. Guard the system of laws, consider carefully and selflessly how it might be added to or amended before it is changed. Protect the laws that protect all.

The discussion must go on. Let the discussion continue my friends. For considering rightfully the positions of all is the key to keeping a country of freedom and openness, that will maintain our country in respectful egis to care for all. To do less is to become the modern equivalent of Segesta, a people without communal direction and value who not only do not respect self-beliefs but do not consider the rights and beliefs of others.

Made in the USA
Charleston, SC
17 September 2014